Pocket Prayer Book

Excerpts from Divine Accordance

Holly Burger

Paperback Version
Copyright © 2007, 2012, 2017
Lightworkers Alliance®, Art-a-Fire®
Holly Burger
Longmont, Colorado
ISBN: 978-0-9838551-0-1

All Rights Reserved
No part of this book may be reproduced, transmitted, copied, scanned, digitally stored or photocopied without permission in writing from author/publisher.

For more information:
www.LightworkersAlliance.com
holly@lightworkersalliance.com

Table of Contents

Table of Contents	5
Vertical Alignment Prayer	11
Prayer for Setting Space	12
Divine Accordance Prayer	13
Release Protocol	14
Prayer for Protection	15
Choose to Remember	16
Heart Protection Prayer	16
Highest Source of Light	17
Prayer for Centering	18
Closing Prayer	19
Closing the Space Prayer	20
Sustenance Prayer for Addiction	21
Prayer for Lightworkers	22
Creation Divine	23
Prayer for Balance	24
Prayer for New Knowledge	25
Prayer for Positive Thinking	26
Willingness to Heal Prayer	27
Prayer for Someone Ill	28
Vertical Soul Integration	29

Prayer for Help With Fear	30
Release of Burden	31
Understanding Karma Prayer	32
Bath of Light Prayer	33
Release and Clearing Space Prayer	34
Genetic Filtration	35
Responsibility and Protocol	35
Grounding Prayer	36
Light Anchor Visualization	37
Sleeping Prayer	39
Sleeping & Prevention of Negative Astral Travel	40
Safe Sleep Prayer	41
Release Violence from the Past	42
Prayer to Disconnect From & Forgive the Past	44
Forgiveness & Empowerment through Uncond. Love	45
Discord Prayer	46
Interpretation Prayer	47
Appreciate Self Prayer	47
Be Present with Your Presence Prayer	48
Manifestation Prayer	49
Understand Manifestation Prayer	50
Witness yourSelf as a Creator	51
Clear Mind Consciousness	52
Knowledge, Wisdom & Understanding	53
Embrace Self Prayer	54
Prosperity Prayer	55
Juggling Frequencies	56
Receive Light Prayer	57
Receive Blessings Prayer	58

Relocation Prayer	59
Transition Prayer	62
Mourning	63
Prayer for Finding the Arms of God	64
Prayer for Gratitude	65
Thanks Giving	66
Index	71

About this book:

Pocket Prayer Book is a compilation of prayers and exercises given to me by spiritual guides during meditation. *Discord Prayer* was the first prayer I received, back in 2001. Feedback encouraged me, so I continued writing the sacred words with healing powers, printing and sharing them freely. With pieces of paper everywhere organization was necessary. The first book was put together in 2006; a spiral bound pamphlet named *Divine Accordance* after one of my favorite prayers. That first incarnation included a descriptive paragraph with each prayer. People wanted to know how to work with the prayers, where they came from and more. I expanded the small paragraphs into chapters and *Divine Accordance* became a book. The little book became *Pocket Prayer Book, Excerpts from Divine Accordance*.

Prayers begin with Father, Mother, God/Goddess, Creator, Source of All That Is, which is my attempt to please all belief systems. If I missed yours, please substitute or adjust words to accommodate your views.

Most importantly, I want to thank you for being your true essence and spreading your Light. I hope that this little book brings you as much joy and healing as it has given me over the years.

With gratitude, love and appreciation,

Holly

Vertical Alignment Prayer

Father/Mother/God/Goddess, Creator, Source of All That Is; I call forth to the highest frequencies of Light. Please help me access my internal flame.

I allow my internal Light to nourish and replenish me. I am blessed through Divine channels, I am loved.

Please assist me, help me connect with my High-Self and the I Am Presence.

I am One with Divine Light.

Please assist me further, help me ground and connect with Gaia and Earth in the most appropriate way.

I am One with my planet, Earth, Gaia.

As a physical conduit, in service to the Divine, I am a Pillar of Light between Gaia and the I Am Presence.

Thank you and Amen.

Prayer for Setting Space

Father, Mother, God, Goddess, Creator, Source of All That Is; please assist us in setting *sacred space* by sealing this area off on the north, south, east, west, above, below and all areas in between.

We invite our guides, angels, ascended masters and all appropriate Beings of Light sent to us by Source; allowing only those Beings that are one-hundred percent pure Christ Consciousness frequency or higher, the most advanced forms of truth and unconditional love to assist us.

Please further assist us in grounding and connecting to Gaia in the most appropriate way for our work today. Please strengthen and repair our grounding cords if necessary. As we feel the connection to Gaia, we embrace our agreements and allow the energy to return to our physical bodies.

Via our Crystalline Cords of Light, help us connect to our High-Selves, and then the I Am Presence (Source). Please strengthen and repair the cord if necessary. As we align with Source we offer ourselves in service to the Divine, working with the highest and best good of all involved.

In this surrender and alignment with Source, we allow guidance, protection and love from Source and those sent by Source.

Thank you and Amen.

Divine Accordance Prayer

Father, Mother, God, Goddess, Creator, Source of All That Is; I offer myself in surrender to the Divine Will of God and ask that my work and communication be governed by this surrender. It is commanded by my client* and me that our work be for the highest and best good of all involved.

We allow only those Beings that are one-hundred percent pure Christ Consciousness frequency or higher, the most advanced forms of truth and unconditional love to assist us.

We ask that all communication be Oversoul-to-Oversoul or higher. Please assist us in putting aside mind, ego and personality so that information can come through in a clear and concise manner, as accurately as possible.

In this surrender and alignment with Source, we allow guidance, protection and love from Source and those sent by Source.

Thank you and Amen.

*be sure to ask client for permission

Release Protocol

Father, Mother, God, Goddess, Creator, Source of All That Is; with gratitude, appreciation and love, we ask that all things released during this session (work, prayer, massage) be surrounded with Light and taken onto their own highest outworkings. Please heal and seal all exits and entrances used by any negative force or negative entity in any field, level or layer of existence.

Please help us to release any energies, frequencies or thoughts that have attracted negativity in any form. We ask for assistance in holding a vertical frequency of Light, or the most appropriate alignment, as we heal, surrender and release.

Please teach us to hold the frequencies of Light available to us, as we align further with the truth of whom and what we are.

I clearly see: I Am Light.

Thank you and Amen.

Prayer for Protection

Father, Mother, God, Goddess, Creator, Source of All That Is; please send forth a complete, safe and unfractured container of Light to surround me sealed off on the north, south, east, west, above and below. Please see that I am connected to Source and to Earth so that I may know my own presence as I know yours, Father/Mother/God/Goddess.

Please see that I am not compromised at any level or at any frequency. I ask for an invincible barrier of protection, shielding and guidance to be sent from my highest source of Light, where truth and only truth are allowed, I accept no other. Please help me to release negative energy, thought forms, entities, blocks, ideas or anything not serving my highest good and escort these out of my safe container of Light.

I ask for assistance in cutting all cords, around, above and below me. Please turn any negative energy I am responsible for into love and please turn any negative energy directed towards me into love. I know that as I say this it is true. I offer my most gracious thanks to all who work with me.

Thank you and Amen.

Choose to Remember

I choose to remember with grace and ease. I release judgment of all others and myself for putting the veils of incarnation in place. My life and experiences are guided by love. I design my learning openly with a heart full of Light.

I Am, I remember.

Thank you and Amen.

Heart Protection Prayer

I allow Source energy to protect, guard and guide me through all experiences in my life. I surrender my ego to Divine Will and know that I am the Light and love that I crave.

I allow the Christ Consciousness flame to burn brightly within me and throughout all of my bodies. As my heart energy expands, and my love grows I know that I am protected.

Thank you and Amen.

Highest Source of Light

I command now, on behalf of myself, guidance from Father, Mother, God, Goddess, Creator, Source of all That Is. When I pray, let it be known that I am protected by the Highest Light Source and guided by the same. My communication in prayer and meditation is through the most advanced form of light, from me to the Highest Source of Light known to me as God. My protection aligns me with the highest light and unconditional love of the Divine I Am Presence.

Thank you and Amen.

Prayer for Centering

Father, Mother, God, Goddess, Creator, Source of All That Is; in this moment I call forth assistance to help me center.

I let go of my day, my worries and concerns.

I release all that I think is important to my guides and angels, and I accept their help.

I allow the Light of God/Goddess to open within me and clear me of all that is less than pure Light. With this Light, I release distraction and burden, I embrace love and healing. My doubts and insecurities are replaced with knowledge and strength.

I welcome peace. I am calm. I am relaxed.

I welcome alignment; I AM connected to Source and grounded to Earth.

I AM centered.

Thank you and Amen.

Closing Prayer

We wish to thank all Beings of Light that have assisted us today as we release them back to their realms of choice. We ask that Source bless them with the highest frequencies of love, appreciation and gratitude on our behalf.

We disconnect from all those we have invoked through name or frequency and ask that they be blessed with light, love and appreciation through the light of God/Goddess.

We release ourselves back to our third-dimensional expression, where we choose to be the forward expression of Light, and ask for assistance in grounding.

We disconnect from each other, the Akashic Records and the Oversoul; and release our *sacred space*. We ask that there be no transference and that all information be received through each person's own discernment.

Thank you and Amen.

Closing the Space Prayer

I wish to thank all of the guides, angels, ascended masters and Beings of Light that have joined me today for this meditation*. As they release back to their realms of choice I ask that Source please bless these Beings with the highest frequencies of love, appreciation and gratitude on my (our) behalf.

I ask that Source please release and close the *sacred space*. I ask that all those invoked by name or thought be blessed and any cords or inappropriate energy connections be severed and healed. Please keep me grounded and connected to Source, in my Pillar of Light.

Thank you and Amen.

*session, group, massage, healing work, etc.

Sustenance Prayer for Addiction

Father, Mother, God, Goddess, Creator, Source of All That Is; please assist me; I am willing to absorb LIGHT so that I may heal. I am willing to release any frequency less than one-hundred percent unconditional love causing me to use any source for less than optimal advantage.

If I partake in anything out of habit I ask, command and allow that all negative frequencies from that source be immediately transformed to Light, and all positive frequencies from that source be utilized by my High-Self for my highest and best good.

To all engineering forces that guide my desires, cravings or focus: I release you into the LIGHT. I allow my will to be the will of God/Goddess. I allow clarity from my guidance concerning addiction. I allow wholeness, goodness, health and balance to be my goals and manifest SELF.

Thank you and Amen.

(Note: The words 'forces that guide' refer to entities or negative energies that might be influencing your thoughts or actions.)

Prayer for Lightworkers

Father, Mother, God, Goddess, Creator, Source of All That Is; I offer myself in service to the Light. I am in surrender; God's will be done. Thy will is my will, we are One. Please, see that I am complete on all levels, vibrations and frequencies, and in all bodies. If I am fragmented from any part of my Self, I command and demand those fragments to return now in complete form with no alteration or additions.

Please remove anything dark or negative from any of my bodies or aspects of myself, known or unknown to me, and return these to their creator. In asking that this is done, I know it is so.

I ask for assistance in my Lightwork and in all aspects of my life and growth. Please guide me to do what is in accordance with my Divine plan. Please assist me in staying in my heart center and using Spirit as a guide. It is my intention to work and listen to pure Christ Consciousness Light and only Christ Consciousness Light.

Thank you and Amen.

Creation Divine

Blessed be the inspirations that feed our minds and hearts. Through them, we create motivation and desire. We call forth to Source Light inspiration and offer ourselves in service.

God/Goddess awaken our Lights to their true purpose. Align our senses to Divine Knowledge and Truth. Let our service become Universal Law. Those who serve as one create as one.

Creation Divine, Creation Pure, Will of All, The Absolute, Source; guide us to the path of enrichment and consciousness as our hearts, minds, bodies, Spirits and Souls remember oneness, responsibility and truth.

We recognize that thought begets and forgives. We are One, unified and creating together through intention and action. As One, "I love, I forgive, I Am."

Thank you and Amen.

Prayer for Balance

God, grant me vision to see that everything placed in front of me is from Spirit so that I may embrace every happening and every moment in my life as a gift.

Grant me memory to use when I think I am doing something; help me to remember it is the Oneness of all that truly does the work.

God, please help me remember that I am the Oneness, all power that moves through me is a sign of my investment in the purpose of my life and the intention of my purpose is to be the perfect expression of the will of God, which is truly the will of all, and therefore my will.

God, please continue in your valiant efforts, which are my efforts, to bring surrender into my heart, mind and body so that I may experience the Spirit of all in this physical manifestation.

God, I pray that I can uphold my end of the bargain by completely forgetting all of my ideas and remember that each perfect moment is another example of an expression of the highest teaching and the highest truth.

Let me see opportunity to forgive and to know that forgiveness comes from my heart easily and ceaselessly for all I encounter and, with all my power, for myself.

Let my love and forgiveness for myself become the beacon that others see, and let that beacon lead them to their own awareness of self-love.

Thank you and Amen

Prayer for New Knowledge

Father, Mother, God, Goddess, Creator, Source of All That Is; I request assistance to understand the evolution of knowledge. Please assist me in releasing any blocks to learning and comprehending. Please assist me in accepting all wisdom and learning pertaining to new knowledge. I pray for understanding while my mind releases and my connection to Source gains strength. I accept all this as an example of further truth that we are all One.

I allow my mind, body and Spirit to integrate knowledge, wisdom and understanding from all sources of one-hundred percent pure Christ Consciousness Light, truth and unconditional love. I acknowledge myself as guided, guarded and protected on my journey.

Thank you and Amen.

Prayer for Positive Thinking

Father, Mother, God, Goddess, Creator, Source of All That Is; it is my intention to think positive, expressive, helpful thoughts. Be it known now that I Am increasing my positive energy in every moment.

I Am an expression of positive thinking. I Am a reflection of positive thinking. I Am a magnet for positive thinking. I welcome and enjoy positive thinking. I love positive thinking.

My thoughts reflect my positive self-image and esteem. My smile spreads positive emotions and confidence. I Am positive. Be it so, through my own self-empowerment I grant myself grace, and bless myself into the new me... positive!

Thank you and Amen.

Willingness to Heal Prayer

(fill in blank with what you wish to heal from)

Source Light, through my Divine manifestation I have managed to produce _____. I am no longer in denial. I embrace _____ as the sacred messenger it is.

As _____ teaches me, I release _____ from any further obligation to be with me. I command my body to recognize its ability to be free of _____.

I am willing myself to heal. I open my heart and Soul to the Divine origination of my perfection. Like a fine machine, I open myself to operating perfectly. I allow myself care and cooperation in this endeavor.

I am healthy, healed and awake. I am astounded, amazed and surprised at my ability to heal quickly. I am alive, loved, embraced and guided. I am One.

Thank you and Amen.

Prayer for Someone Ill

(Please insert the appropriate name.)

Father, Mother, God, Goddess, Creator, Source of All That Is; we ask for assistance for _____. Please bless her with harmony of heart, to endure her path. Please bless her with peace of mind, to understand. Please help her eyes shine with God's Light so that all who love _____ see her inner peace and beauty.

We pray for _____'s pain-free recovery. We visualize her good health and joyous future. We acknowledge her as God's child, a child that is loved and cared for by an army of Angels, a wealth of Light.

Through the Light of God let our prayers be answered, let _____ heal.

Thank you and Amen.

Vertical Soul Integration

Father, Mother, God, Goddess, Creator, Source of All That Is; I call upon Divine Will, Source Light and the Alignment of Christ Consciousness Frequency. Please assist me, I ask for a Soul clearing and healing. Please remove any negative attributes or attachments from any Soul integration I have experienced. Please clean, clear and heal my Soul now. Help me to ground all appropriate energies, and release what no longer serves my Light. Please help me to relate to my Soul in its entire expanse and recognize what I have chosen to work with at this time.

I allow Soul Integrations through Divine Light, Divine Will and via Christ Consciousness Frequency. I ask and allow my guides and angels, my High-Self committee and Ascended Masters to assist me in all awakenings concerning my Soul or any aspect of my Self, known or unknown to me.

I ask that this work be done through all time, space and dimension. I command this work to be done peacefully, easily and comfortably.

Thank you and Amen.

Prayer for Help With Fear

Father, Mother, God, Goddess, Creator, Source of All That Is; please assist me in discovering why I fear* _____. I am willing to look at the beginning of this fear*. I am willing to release the root cause of this fear*. I wholeheartedly ask my guides to bring forth any and all help concerning my fear* of _____.

I allow this work peacefully, easily and comfortably according to my highest and best good.

Thank you and Amen.

*If you are experiencing anxiety, agitation, etc. change the word fear to experience.

Release of Burden

Father, Mother, God, Goddess, Creator, Source of All That Is; with Divine Accordance I call forth to God force frequencies of Light for release of all burdens. Through this release, I request karmic healing for all my lineages of Light; past, present and future.

Please assist all bodies in understanding only real, current and true responsibilities. As I gain perspective of my possibilities, I release all burdens from the past, present and future.

I embrace all gifts from past occurrences and release all burdens. I allow all burdens, responsibilities and anger to filter from my mind. Help me open to resolution.

Furthermore, I release all mental body patterns holding me in a place of stagnation or accumulation of negative energy. I release old patterns and clear resentment, burden and overwhelm. I welcome love, Light and understanding to integrate with all my God-given gifts. My chosen reality is here. I am free, I am abundant, I am well.

Thank you and Amen.

Understanding Karma Prayer

Father, Mother, God, Goddess, Creator, Source of All That Is; please assist me in realizing all reasons for my interaction with _____*. It is my full intention to participate in any outworking that is my design; peacefully, easily and comfortably. Through my empowerment to create I call forth Source to assist me in creating with responsibility and kindness to my Self and others.

I ask that I be blessed with understanding that will help me feel grateful and appreciative towards those teaching me through all karmic experiences. I allow agitation and fear to be transmuted by Light while I embrace unconditional love for all those assisting my life on this planet.

Thank you and Amen.

*Use name of person, company, feeling, place, etc.

Bath of Light Prayer

Beloved Presence, I have offered my assistance in service to the Divine, now I request clearing and balancing.

-Please, align all new energies to integrate in a comfortable manner. (Pause for this to happen.)

-Please, help me release what I have unlocked, completely, including anything hidden or sub-conscious.

-Please, align all my bodies to my vertical Pillar of Light.

I recognize now: I am an evolution. I am safe in change. I am a welcome aspect of Light in my community and among my friends and family.

My old attachments are freely released for transmutation.

In my new freedom, I am _____. (Insert your own words here.)

I am comfortable with my changes. My self-expression is also an evolution.

I welcome my new reflection in the world.

I am a Divine Carrier of Light. I am a Divine Healer and I Am Divinely healed.

Thank you and Amen.

Release and Clearing Space Prayer

Father, Mother, God, Goddess, Creator, Source of All That Is; I acknowledge the sacred, Divine Light that I carry within. I allow this Light to grow larger, greater, wider, and brighter until it encompasses my entire body. Within this Light, I command the clearing of all frequencies less than one-hundred percent Christ Consciousness Light. Please release and clear anything causing fear or stress, within or around my body, to the Light.

HOME or OFFICE: I ask that sacred, Divine Light continue to grow clearing this space, room and building. I call forth to the High-Self of the owner of this building and ask permission for this clearing. I call forth to the Soul of this building for permission and assistance. Please clear all inanimate objects connected to this home/office, building or property.

CAR: I ask that the Light continue to grow, clearing this vehicle, and objects within, of all negativity. Please adjust all electrical currents and do whatever is necessary to keep this car protected safe and in perfect working order.

ALL: I allow this work to follow Divine Accordance; working with the highest good for all and surrender to Divine Will. I command everything released into the Light or highest out-workings.

Thank you and Amen.

Genetic Filtration

Through the Light of God, I ask for assistance in filtering all lineage transfers. Please create a filter so that all transfers happen through Source. My High-Self is the guardian of all receptors concerning lineage transfer, energy and genetic pattern. Let this be so through the Highest Source of Light and Truth in the most appropriate form. With grace and ease, I allow this change. With comfort and appropriate timing, I allow resolution. It is so.

Thank you and Amen.

Responsibility and Protocol

We are the Divine Creators of our realities. Everything we see is a mirror, a reflection of what is inside of us. We attract all situations, happenings, conversations, events and circumstances. We understand the Law of Attraction. We know we are not separate from God/Goddess, but part of the One. We are healing and healed. We walk a path of Light. We are pure, open and awake.

Thank you and Amen.

Grounding Prayer

Father/Mother/God/Goddess, Creator, Source of All That Is; please assist me in grounding and connecting deeply with Earth and Gaia. I ask for assistance in grounding as appropriate for my highest and best good. I command all negative and/or interfering energies/entities to be surrounded with Light and taken on to their highest out-workings. I offer myself in service to Divine Light, Source of all that Is and allow myself to be the highest expression of Light possible.

Thank you and Amen.

Light Anchor Visualization

In a quiet, comfortable place, prepare for meditation. Ask your guides to help you visualize and experience the following exercise.

Place your hands over your high heart, it is between your throat and physical heart. Take a deep breath and focus on your high heart. Imagine that there is a glowing light within. Feel the Light of Source expand within your chest. Feel beautiful, bright, clear golden Light.

Imagine that the pure golden Light becomes an anchor within your high heart. Feel it as it becomes very heavy. Feel the weight of your anchor pulled by gravity. As you let the anchor descend, you see an ever-lengthening golden Light cord extending from your high heart.

The anchor seems to gain heaviness as Earth pulls it with gravity. You can feel your anchor move as it is guided by Source to the core of Earth. Feel it move through rock, sediment, water. It disturbs nothing; it is disturbed by nothing. Feel your anchor of Light move directly to the center of Earth, to the great Light waiting for you there.

If you lose your way, do not worry. Source is guiding and Earth is receiving. Release your ideas of completion and allow your natural connection to awaken. Feel your Pillar of

(continued)

Light protecting you, your guides showing you the way. Sense the great Light at the core of Earth. Ground, connect.

Remember:

Between Earth and Source, we exist in a Pillar of Light. Feel this connection daily. Let the knowledge become natural for you.

It is from this place we manifest. If your truest desire is to be who you are, know yourself as a vast Light, perfect in creation, full of wisdom and love.

Thank you and Amen.

Sleeping Prayer

Father, Mother, God, Goddess, Creator, Source of All That Is; please help me sleep tonight. It is my intention to wake at _____a.m. rested, rejuvenated and rejoicing! I allow my Self this time of conscious release and surrender. I invoke Christ Consciousness Light within and allow it to amplify through all my bodies, levels and areas of existence. I call forth the Almighty Presence of God to assist me in any way possible so that I may sleep soundly and comfortably on this night.

Thank you and Amen.

Sleeping & Prevention of Negative Astral Travel

From this body and this mind, I state clearly it is my intention to sleep soundly tonight. I call forth Archangel Michael and Christ Consciousness Light to ask for assistance, please repair any damage to the crystalline cord and structure that connect me to Source. Please repair any damage to the grounding cord and structure that connect me to Earth.

It is my intention to sleep each night and wake rested and revived. I allow my cosmic physician to repair and heal all aspects of my being during my sleep. I allow and accept help from Beings that are the one-hundred percent pure unconditional love during my sleep state.

I ask for *spiritual transcendence* for my Soul and all aspects of my Soul at all levels, realities and positions.

I allow Spirit to guide me on my journey. It is my intention to allow healing, knowledge, wisdom and understanding to infiltrate my consciousness and bodies. I allow all that is guided by Source and surrender myself to Divine Will.

Thank you and Amen.

Safe Sleep Prayer

Father, Mother, God, Goddess, Creator, Source of All That Is; I call forth the original spark of love that is the highest form of truth. I allow this ultimate form of Light to be my guide. From this moment forward, I will call this Light, in its most advanced form, Source. I allow this Light to continually advance and grow. I allow it to bless and teach me. As I learn about love, I will remember who I am and know myself as the Divine Spark that I Am.

I allow Source to show me Light. I allow Source to show me trust. I allow Source to show me faith. I am the ever-deserving witness and believer in the divinity of Source and Oneness that warrant me love and protection.

Source, tonight show me a safe way to sleep. Show me peace and beauty in the form of a sacred garden. A garden surrounded by an impenetrable fence, secured with a gate only I can open. Within this garden, love and life bloom. I am safe in the high frequencies of Christ Consciousness Light that protect this garden. My garden resides in the dimensions of Light that no darkness can penetrate. When I close my eyes, I trust that Source, Creator of All Light will take me to my sacred garden and watch over my deep, restful sleep.

When I wake, I will be rested, rejuvenated and joyful. Let this prayer be my voice, my choice and my reality. From this moment forward, I command my own recognition of the Light force that dwells within me. From that Light force, I say, so it is. Thank you and Amen.

Release Violence from the Past

Father, Mother, God, Goddess, Creator, Source of All That Is; I ask, in this moment, to be cleared of any frequencies that resonate with violence from this life or any other life. I ask that I be cleared thru all levels of Light, through all dimensions and all space. I ask for karma to be released, cleared or completed that has to do with violence, assault, aggression or anger. I ask that I be released and cleared of all grief concerning any experience with violence. I ask that peaceful messages come upon me and that I be gently guided to a form of release that is appropriate for me.

I ask that I be empowered to understand that I can release, that there is a place where these things are held and it is not within my physical body. I ask for help in knowing that there are guardians of these archives and they will help me to move through these changes peacefully, easily and comfortably.

In the gentleness that I create for myself, I ask that Source remind me, as long as it takes, over and over again, that I am in a peaceful existence. I release any energies of guilt or shame that cause me to deny myself a peaceful existence. I allow all violent frequencies to move past me without my notice and if possible into the Light.

(continued)

I ask that my Light attract Light and that my mind recognize that my dominant force is Light, that I am One with Source on this planet and I create peace, ease and comfort. I create love, healing, happiness. Even if I witness otherwise, I command that my mind recognize it is only something I see. Let it be known now that I do not have to experience everything to know it. As I learn through all experiences, I am more aware, I am more conscious, I am more awake.

My gratitude to all who help me on this journey, thank you and Amen.

Prayer to Disconnect From & Forgive the Past

Divine beloved Creator that I Am, my movements on this planet and in this life are completely understood through my High-Self.

I release now resentment of any plans, actions or happenings that have brought about pain or discomfort at any time, via any experience.

From this moment forward, I create learning peacefully, easily and comfortably, for my Divine self and my third-dimensional self.

I allow realization to happen. I release old habits of learning the hard way. I discontinue patterns of sabotage, abuse, neglect, abandonment, fear, loneliness, lack of confidence or failure.

I embrace friendship, love and safety in relationships. I am healed from all past happenings that resulted in hardship, suffering, sadness, misunderstanding, unhappiness, distress or any other discordant energy. I now welcome trust, faith and joy.

My heart, mind, body, Soul and Spirit forgive my creations of pain and those who participated, including my Self. I completely release any energetic obligation from any person or circumstance I have used to learn without love and acceptance. I accept full responsibility for my existence. I am loved, nurtured, cared for and I welcome me as I Am.

Thank you and Amen.

Forgiveness & Empowerment through Unconditional Love

Fully, your heart open, know yourself to be a Divine Creation! Fully, your heart aware, see no separation.

Upon abandoning what you think is real, you have only Light to guide you back to the pure place of no description. Forgiveness for your travels, your choices, forgiveness Divine.

Expect your enlightened neighbor; expect your masterful friends; believe the Law of Attraction; see your manifestation.

Remember, as a blessing you've earned through a thousand lifetimes, a million Soul agreements. Be your own witness. Let the critic die. Let evolution recreate, rebirth your own inner negativity into Divine Service, Divine Witness, Divine Love.

Be it known – the heart is open, love is welcome. Present ever, beyond the air you breathe and ground you traverse upon, Divine Unconditional Love reigns.

Call upon it, as if it were a butterfly to alight, a dream to visit, call upon it.

Thank you and Amen.

Discord Prayer

On this day, I feel discord with you. I release this discord. I release all negative energy concerning it. I sever all energy cords I have sent to you and all energy cords you have sent to me; completely, above, below and around. I withdraw all energy I have inflated in any situation, conversation, past life or current life occurrence with you.

I forgive you for everything. I forgive myself, for everything.

As the God/Goddess that I Am, I turn all negative energy I have sent to you into love. As the God/Goddess that I Am, I turn all negative energy you have directed towards me into love.

I accept only love from you and offer only love to you. I send you blessings for all the lessons you represent and wholeheartedly accept them. I release you from any further obligation I have created that could bring negativity into my life, or yours. I allow myself to see the role we have both played in this learning and thank you for helping me see that I Am a whole being of loving Light, and that I choose to learn in a loving and caring way.

Thank you and Amen.

Interpretation Prayer

Father, Mother, God, Goddess, Creator, Source of All That Is; I call forth your assistance in understanding my interaction with _____. Please help me understand the meaning of all words and actions, from all participants in this situation including myself. Please help me see why I created this and what I intend to learn. I allow all anger, jealousy, shame and resentment to evaporate with this understanding. I Am love. I Am Light.

Thank you and Amen.

Appreciate Self Prayer

Father, Mother, God, Goddess, Creator, Source of All That Is; show me the way to self-appreciation. I ask for assistance in seeing and understanding my value. As I walk this path of learning that I Am, please help me to release anything in the way. Please show me where I shine and how I Am an aspect of the Divine orce that holds all. As I Am in service to the Light, help me to feel forgiveness when I am harsh to others or myself. Please assist this release on all levels, through all time and space.

Thank you and Amen.

Be Present with Your Presence Prayer

Divine Creator, in this moment I ask that my mind be balanced so that I may see my service. Show me how to be present with the presence within. I welcome gentle reminders to love my neighbor, to forgive my judgments, to remember my service.

As I bow before the mirror, please help me to remember Oneness. As I kneel before poverty, help me to know my abundance starts within and I am free of restraints. I am limitless.

As I recognize wholeness, I see that I am whole. As I seek wholeness, I know that I am whole.

Divine Creator of all that is, I welcome assistance. Help me know my heart, to forgive the ways of the lost, even if they are my ways. I am in truth, I am truth. I shine truth from the Oneness that I Am.

Blessed are those that reflect the truth, for they are me and I am them. We are One. Divine truth reigns free, upon my heart burdens are lifted and I Am free.

In gratitude for the abundant blessings that make up my life, Amen.

Manifestation Prayer

Father, Mother, God, Goddess, Creator, Source of All That Is; I follow my heart's desire. I allow my inner vision to be the map that brings my desire to a clear and present reality. I allow lesser frequencies to rest without my attention. I see Light, and I only react to what is appropriate for my growth and desires. In this, I see that Divine Order is simple and gratifying. In this, I see that Light will lead me to comfort and possibility.

I allow my manifestation ability to be guided by God, Divine Will and my desire to be One with all. I allow comfort and nurturing, trust and conscientiousness to be mine. As this manifests and grows, I release judgment about how it arrives. I smile, I feel warm, I am loved. I am nurtured, I am trusted, I am well. My process, my lessons arrive and are experienced peacefully, easily and comfortably. Therefore, as I Am that I Am, I accept my developing abilities of manifestation as the Divine Will of God/Goddess/Creator.

Thank you and Amen.

Understand Manifestation Prayer

Father, Mother, God, Goddess, Creator, Source of All That Is; please assist me in understanding my creations.

My full awareness is opening. I am able to see how and why I create the life I live. Angels and guides from Source are assisting me in this understanding. I am currently experiencing the Divine Order of my creative talents.

As my opportunities to learn unfold peacefully, easily and comfortably, I embrace each one with an open heart. I am supported in witnessing the current situation I call 'my life.' I am supported in all ideas of change and improvement. These ideas and implementations will be for my highest good, or they will be forgotten.

Therefore, what I forget, I release. What I remember, I embrace. In the Divine Light that I Am, I allow Source Light to express unconditional love, forgiveness and spiritual empowerment through me.

Thank you and Amen.

Witness yourSelf as a Creator

Father, Mother, God, Goddess, Creator, Source of All That Is; I allow Light to bless all those I love, including my Self! I am willingly in surrender and service to my original Source of Light. I allow blessings and reminders of this Light to be abundant in my life. I allow all things blocking my memory of Source to leave now; I choose to remember. I allow my existence to be the only example I need that I am One with God/Goddess/Creator. I easily move into a peaceful experience and allow Christ Consciousness energy to envelop me, nurture me, and help me see who I Am.

As I continue to experience love and release fear in this physical expression I allow my Self to be the forward expression of Light.

Thank you and Amen.

Clear Mind Consciousness

Father, Mother, God, Goddess, Creator, Source of All That Is; I call forth the highest frequencies of Light to release all burdens, encumbrances, entities and parasitical influences.

Please send forth all things appropriate for me to reach clear mind consciousness. I am a willing servant to the Light. I banish all frequencies less than one-hundred percent unconditional Christ Consciousness Light.

I release my mind's idea of clarity and protection and receive my Creator's. I accept in place of all mental body ideas and influences Divine intention, Divine knowledge, wisdom and understanding, Divine love.

My love is the conduit from which I receive. As I am, my existence explains my ability, probability and capability of receiving Creator's love. I am a living, breathing example of the perfection of Divine love. I heal myself through the presence of the eternal heart flame that I Am. I balance all bodies and existences through all times and places, I allow peace to be my emission, love to be my example and Light to be my existence. I Am.

By the power of creation, I now decree my life as guided, guarded and protected by the love God/Goddess/Creator. I am guided by Divine Will and those directed by Divine Will. I am guarded by the vertical energy known as my Pillar of Light extending between Source and the core of Earth. I am protected by Light, as is my right according to Universal Law.

Thank you and Amen.

Knowledge, Wisdom & Understanding

Father, Mother, God, Goddess, Creator, Source of All That Is; I request assistance in filling my heart's need. I request knowledge, wisdom and understanding concerning _____. Please assist me in locating, discovering, acknowledging all wisdom and learning concerning _____ in my life and around me.

Source, help me understand this knowledge and wisdom so that my mind can release and my connection to Divinity can strengthen. I allow all this as further truth that we are all One.

I allow my mind, body and Spirit to integrate knowledge, wisdom and understanding from all sources of one-hundred percent Christ Consciousness Light and unconditional love.

I am guided, guarded and protected on my journey.

Thank you and Amen.

Embrace Self Prayer

I am clearing and releasing and I love it! I love my cleansed body, my youthful, healthy self! I embrace the ease and comfort from which I think, live and breathe.

My comforts are many. My friends are many. My beloved SELF exemplifies worth, love and empowerment.

Through all that I Am I seek TRUTH, LOVE, LIGHT.

I embrace unconditional love and all aspects of Light that I Am.

Thank you and Amen.

Prosperity Prayer

Father, Mother, God, Goddess, Creator, Source of All That Is; I ask for assistance with prosperity. From this moment on, I allow my prosperity to be in the hands of the Divine. I ask that any form of attachment to my ability to manifest that is not in Divine Accordance* be immediately severed. I ask that all forms of manifestation that I have in any way participated in, be either removed from my being or returned to my being, whichever is for my highest good.

I allow myself to experience all forms of prosperity, but particularly money. I allow cash flow and welcome disposable income without judgment of where it comes from, how it arrives or how I will spend it.

If any form of my energy is stalled, trapped or stagnant concerning prosperity, I ask that Beings of one-hundred percent pure Christ Consciousness Light assist me in releasing, disconnecting, claiming, motivating or taking most appropriate action so that I may experience continued prosperity and abundance.

Creator, Source, as I grow and expand, as I raise my frequency I ask that this work, or more appropriate work following Divine Accordance Prayer, be done to increase my ability to prosper financially with integrity and responsibility. I welcome new aspects of abundance; I welcome all forms of love and Light, including the form of money.

Thank you and Amen.

Juggling Frequencies

Father, Mother, God, Goddess, Creator, Source of All That Is; it is my intention to move forward in my chosen third-dimensional expression as an example of unconditional love. I allow any pattern, thought form, frequency or interference that can be changed to accommodate and accept unconditional love to be changed now.

For myself, I allow further understanding and compassion so that my journey on Earth is a walk of peace. I ask for protection for all bodies, levels, planes and aspects that make me who I Am.

Let this protection come in the highest, most advanced form of Light. Let it begin within me and move out to others in the form of unconditional love. I allow myself to be an example of Light, good health and joy. I release any programs, ideas, thoughts, past lives, occurrences or influences that restrict my connection to God/Creator/Source. As Light fills my expanse, replacing what I have released, I remember that I Am the very spark that began all of creation.

By the power of all that I Am, I declare myself free of negative influences, free of negative interference, free of energies carrying less than one-hundred percent Christ Consciousness Frequency. I proceed guided by Divine Will as an example of Light, unconditional love, balance, good health and joy.

Thank you and Amen.

Receive Light Prayer

Father, Mother, God, Goddess, Creator, Source of All That Is;

-I allow Light to bless all those I love, including mySELF!

-I am willingly in surrender and service to my original Source of Light.

-I allow blessings and reminders of this Light to be abundant in my life.

-I allow everything blocking my memory of Source to leave now, I choose to remember.

-I allow my existence to be the only example I need that I am One with God/Goddess/Creator.

I easily move into a peaceful experience and allow Christ Consciousness energy to envelop me, nurture me and help me see who I Am. As I continue to experience love and release fear in this physical expression, I allow my Self to be the forward expression of Light.

Thank you and Amen.

Receive Blessings Prayer

Father, Mother, God, Goddess, Creator, Source of All That Is; I call forth my Highest Source of Light for this prayer. Please help me to receive blessings that are for my highest and best good. I surrender my will, ideas, ego and personality to the Divine Will of God/Goddess/Creator. I allow anything no longer serving me to be released into the Light.

I ask for assistance so that I may receive blessings, including: abundance, good health, happiness, prosperity, self-confidence, JOY, balance, deep rewarding sleep, smiles, LIGHT, love, friends, fun, etc. (I allow my Source/Creator to use "etcetera" as appropriate!)

I initiate blessings in this moment. I welcome blessings from all aspects of Light. I bless all those I love and myself. I bless the planet, its people and dimensions of expression. I bless the Light of God, so that it may expand and create an avenue for blessings into my being. I welcome the Light of the God/Goddess/Creator; I welcome all that is mine. Within this frequency, I embrace Light and I openly allow it to flow from me as an expression of the Divine Force that I Am.

Thank you and Amen

Relocation Prayer

(For those who listen to the call of Gaia and move their lives to anchor Light.)

Father, Mother, God, Goddess, Creator, Source of All That Is; through the kindness of my own true heart I call forth the release of judgment. In my heart, I unify all belief systems. This I call 'Oneness'. I command an echo of the Oneness for my mind and Soul.

I am now familiar with enlightened thinking and I now portray consciousness. My love for the Divine is my love for humanity and every living thing.

My understanding of religion and belief is now taken back to the seed of origination. In the beginning, there was only love. That is all I remember.

I am compassionate and open to my fellow children of Light. As they heal, I heal. As I heal, they heal.

Oneness prevails, I judge not. I am free of the separation; I embrace truth and unconditional love.

I am prepared for God's work as I Am. Any mistakes are forgiven and forgotten. All wounds are healed. I am compassionate and forgiving. I love and I am loved. I forgive and I am forgiven.

I embrace my ethereal brothers and sisters. I lead them to the Light, to understanding, joy and peace.

My awakened heart speaks of love. I am a beacon, a pillar, a sun. Light is anchored through me and I am healed.

(continued)

In my wholeness, I hear the call. I follow my heart, my knowing and I arrive to do my work.

I remember! I remember every step is not measured, I am not judged. My choices are guided, expressed and guided some more.

I am loved! I gather about me support. I shower upon those legions of help my love, adoration, appreciation, gratitude; my Light.

My awakened heart speaks of love. Under any label, religion, race or gender, I love you. Under any façade, lies, corruption, crime, judgment, hate; I forgive you.

I am a Lightworker. Whatever language, location or vocation I am in surrender to the Divine Creator. I will show you and be shown. I will teach you and learn. I will talk and listen. I will be active and rest. I will move, I will live, I will love.

As I visit and experience different places my Light grounds into Earth. Seeds of love from my heart are planted. When I am gone, these seeds grow; they flower and reseed.

Many lifetimes, here and away, I have given of myself in this way. It is my way. I am the love and peace I seek; even in my pain, even when I can't remember...

I AM LOVE!

My truth vibrates out when I forget to speak it.
My integrity echoes forth when I forget to honor it.

(continued)

My love is seen when I forget who I am.

I AM nurtured, held, loved. I AM fed, sheltered and provided for. I AM guided, guarded and protected.

By the Light that I AM, through my Divine Service, with my free will:

-I AM a directionless feather that floats upon the wind extracted from an ethereal wing.
-I AM a directional beam of Light, focused and true.
-I AM a channel of Light; a voice of Divinity
-I AM at peace in my travels and always home.
-I AM one with my surroundings.
-I AM grounded.
-I AM connected with the I AM Presence.
-I AM expansive; I am serving; I AM served.

Through the Light of Creation, I AM.

My heart beats true with the current of Light that runs like a river through each of us.
One. We are One.
Thank you and Amen.

Transition Prayer

(Angela is used in place of someone's name.)

In me there is a guide, one aware of journeys. I invoke that guide now.

Father, Mother, God, Goddess, Creator, Source of All That Is; safely show my beloved Angela the Light of Transition.

Help her know that I am fine.

My heart aches with loss, my mind is reckless with fear, yet I know she is only taking her place among angels. I will hold her memory, hear her laugh and remember her Light. As I heal, I am comforted in two ways. One, she is with God. Two, she was with me.

My privilege and honor to know Angela will be exemplified by my graceful healing. I am able to feel her always. Through God's grace, she never leaves my heart.

My memory may fade, my body weaken, but my heart will never release the love I have for Angela.

With God, she is. With God, I AM. We are never apart, eternally connected through the Divine Oneness that we are.

Thank you and Amen.

Mourning

Beloved, I miss you. Your body gone, your Spirit alive. I hold on to this physical expression, the one you choose as _____. I revel in your memories. I listen to stories, stare at pictures, I miss you.

I miss myself. The way I was with you. How I felt, what we said, when we touched.

Once more if I could caress your cheek, touch your hand, hear your voice. Would not I give anything?

Beloved, my heart aches today, yet I heal. I only offer these words to inform all, I intend to heal. You would not want me to cry, so I see. I watch a blooming world continue. I watch myself continue.

You would not want my guilt. Therefore, I honor your chosen path, your release, your choice. I extend forgiveness to all, to all.

God's will is helping me heal. I am healing. Oh, how I miss you, oh how I heal.

My beloved, my transitional one.

Amen.

Prayer for Finding the Arms of God

Father, Mother, God, Goddess, Creator, Source of All That Is; today we entrust the body of _____ to Earth. Please assist us by providing a safe place for this body here on Earth. Please bless this gravesite with peace and loving reflection upon a life well lived.

Please help _____ on his/her journey to the Light. Please assist his/her family and friends as they release the body of _____ and embrace the memories, love and happiness he/she has left them.

As God sends Angels of Mercy, we pray _____ accepts them and sees his/her family's own angels so that he/she may embrace the beacon of Light sent to him/her. God, please help _____ remember his/her Oneness, his/her true origin. As he/she releases, we request a line of communication for all who desire.

The Light is ever present and awaits us all.

Thank you and Amen.

Prayer for Gratitude

Father, Mother, God, Goddess, Creator, Source of All That Is; I am so grateful for this gift! I whole-heartedly receive this amazing present. Please bless the giver with the highest frequencies of Love, Light and appreciation on my behalf. I am so grateful for this example of abundance in my life. I am so grateful for the giver, her/his inspiration and action. Through this blessing, I acknowledge my part in this creation. Therefore, as we create together we receive together. As we receive together, we give together.

Thank you and Amen.

Thanks Giving

Divinely guided voice within, I am listening. Open to me and for me. Show me how to speak truth from my heart. Show me how to expand the Oneness that I Am and stay in balance with my surroundings.

My life, my service —they are Divine, an example of true Oneness. I am not a random result of coupling. I have not grown in question. I am not a lie.

I have choice. I am allowing. I am voice! My life is an education. I am an example. I am loved and I love. I am grateful.

My Light shines from within, because my Divine Source exists within. Beyond all time, all measure, I am Light. Never have I been separate.

My gratitude expands now. My love brought me here for this experience. My doubt brought education. My loneliness brought love. My questions, answers. My pain, healing. I am so grateful.

Each time I learn I am young, born again as a spark of yearning, a craving hunger joining like to become part of something glorious.

I speak now. I listen now. I give and receive now. I am open. I am a vessel of the original love and I am grateful. I am so very grateful.

(continued)

    Thanks giving, gratitude in the giving. I have given up my former existence to be here, now. I changed myself to be here now. Yet, I am one with my previous. I am one with my future. I am one with my parallel. I am one with you.

    Peace abounds in my heart and I send it out. Let the wind carry it like a seed today to be shared and if possible, rooted.

    If I am responsible for love, peace, forgiveness, Light —I am grateful. If my seed roots, grows and finds its way back to me, I am grateful.

    We are not different, you and I. We are One. Thank you for your example, your teaching, your love.

    I am grateful.
    I am grateful.
    I am grateful.
    Amen.

Thank you for reading ***Pocket Prayer Book***.

The prayers and exercises in this booklet are excerpts from ***Divine Accordance*** by Holly Burger, a comprehensive tool for engaging with your spiritual growth.

For more information, please check:

www.DivineAccordance.com
www.LightworkersAlliance.com

Namastè, Blessings, Aho, Amen

Index

Appreciate Self Prayer 47
Bath of Light Prayer.. 33
Be Present with Your Presence Prayer 48
Choose to Remember... 16
Clear Mind Consciousness.. 52
Closing Prayer.. 19
Closing the Space Prayer 20
Creation Divine.. 23
Discord Prayer 46
Divine Accordance Prayer 13
Embrace Self Prayer 54
Forgiveness & Empowerment through Uncond. Love .. 45
Genetic Filtration... 35
Grounding Prayer 36
Heart Protection Prayer... 16
Highest Source of Light 17
Interpretation Prayer... 47
Juggling Frequencies 56
Knowledge, Wisdom & Understanding 53
Light Anchor Visualization 37

Manifestation Prayer 49
Mourning 63
Prayer for Balance.. 24
Prayer for Centering 18
Prayer for Finding the Arms of God 64
Prayer for Gratitude... 65
Prayer for Help With Fear 30
Prayer for Lightworkers... 22
Prayer for New Knowledge 25
Prayer for Positive Thinking.. 26
Prayer for Protection... 15
Prayer for Setting Space.. 12
Prayer for Someone Ill 28
Prayer to Disconnect From & Forgive the Past............. 44
Prosperity Prayer 55
Receive Blessings Prayer.. 58
Receive Light Prayer 57
Release and Clearing Space Prayer................................ 34
Release of Burden 31
Release Protocol.. 14
Release Violence from the Past 42
Relocation Prayer... 59
Responsibility and Protocol 35
Safe Sleep Prayer 41
Sleeping & Prevention of Negative Astral Travel........... 40
Sleeping Prayer 39

Sustenance Prayer for Addiction	21
Table of Contents	5
Thanks Giving	66
Transition Prayer	62
Understand Manifestation Prayer	50
Understanding Karma Prayer	32
Vertical Alignment Prayer	11
Vertical Soul Integration	29
Willingness to Heal Prayer	27
Witness yourSelf as a Creator	51

www.ingramcontent.com/pod-product-compliance
Lightning Source LLC
Chambersburg PA
CBHW071412040426
42444CB00009B/2217